Winning Answers to Job Interview Questions for Aspiring Managers and Executives

Lavie Margolin

H. Delilah Business & Career Press

Introduction

So, you aspire to be a manager or executive? Can you interview like a manager or an executive? You may have a good grasp of interviewing in general at this point but you have to understand that you are entering a whole new ballgame. Previous questions posed to you and answers that you provided mainly focused on yourself and your work. How about your ability to lead, delegate and most importantly, meet organizational objectives? Are you a big picture thinker and a problem solver? Can you gain the confidence of the CEO, the board of directors and the top executives with your answers and confidence?

Through *Winning Answers to Job Interview Questions for Aspiring Managers and Executives: Successful Skills Preparation Tips for Management Positions*, you can take your interviewing ability to a whole other level. Read this book and understand not only the questions that you can anticipate on an interview, why those questions are being asked and how to answer most effectively.

You may notice as you read that some questions are really getting at the same point using different words, and that some strategies and sample answers are similar. This is done to help you recognize and feel comfortable with the many ways in which an interviewer may request certain information, and to help you as a job seeker to mentally practice retelling the facts and anecdotes about yourself that you are hoping to share in an interview.

Lavie Margolin

Interview Questions & Answers

How would you fire someone?

<u>Why this question is being asked</u>: If you are put in the position of manager, this is a likely occurrence at some point.

<u>Strategy</u>: Explain how you would follow company protocols and try to make it as comfortable a situation as possible.

<u>Sample answer</u>: *I would check with human resources as to company best practices for managing the situation. I would like to provide the person plenty of time to ask questions and know that he/she is being heard, even if it did not work out in this job. I would explain the things that the person had done right on the job and what things were done poorly and why it would not work out here.*

Do you have a geographic preference?

<u>Why this question is being asked</u>: If it is an international business, there might be several opportunities available and the interviewer would like to know where you would like to be located.

<u>Strategy</u>: "Anywhere!" is a dangerous answer unless you have researched where the company has branches and are truly willing to live in any of those locations.

<u>Sample answer</u>: *I am open to anywhere in North America, with a preference towards the northeast.*

What criteria are you using to choose companies to interview with?

Why this question is being asked: To determine if you have a specific plan in seeking the next job opportunity or if you will take any job.

Strategy: Provide examples of criteria that are relevant to the job you are interviewing for. Specifically mention your interest in that industry.

Sample answer: *I have been accepting interviews with Fortune 500 companies in the advertising industry. I am specifically seeking those organizations that do business overseas, support professional development and encourage teamwork.*

Briefly describe the type of career opportunity you are seeking.

<u>Why this question is being asked</u>: To determine if the job you are interviewing for is a match with your career goals.

<u>Strategy</u>: Focus on responsibilities and opportunities that are relevant to the job you are interviewing for.

<u>Sample answer</u>: *I am seeking an opportunity where I can serve as a team leader in managing client accounts. I would like to be responsible for reporting outcomes to management. I want to help develop strategies to move a company forward.*

What do you think is the most difficult thing about being a manager?

<u>Why this question is being asked</u>: To determine what challenges you have faced/anticipate facing in this role.

<u>Strategy</u>: Provide a challenge relevant to the position, how you've approached it in the past and what was the end result.

<u>Sample answer</u>: *One of the most difficult challenges of being a manager is balancing the demands of executives while maximizing the effectiveness of your employees. I feel the best approach is to make sure that there is a good flow of communication between defining what the executives want as well as delivering your expectations to your team.*

How do you get the best out of people?

<u>Why this question is being asked</u>: To learn how you can best manage your workforce.

<u>Strategy</u>: Stress your ability to maximize the strength of employees, motivate them and support them to do their best.

<u>Sample answer</u>: *I believe in leading by example. There is not something I would ask someone to do that I would not do myself.*

What is the next step in your career?

<u>Why this question is being asked</u>: To learn your plan for career growth and to determine how that relates to the job.

<u>Strategy</u>: Focus on the job and why it is the right fit for your career now.

<u>Sample answer</u>: *I have worked my way up to compete for a senior marketing executive position. I began as a marketing coordinator, grew to a junior marketing rep. and lastly to an account manager. I think this is the next great step for me and I'd look forward to growing in an opportunity like this.*

Describe a team experience you found disappointing.

Why this question is being asked: Not all group experiences will be positive. The interviewer would like to know why a team experience did not work out and how you dealt with it.

Strategy: Provide an example relevant to the job. Explain what the situation was that necessitated teamwork, why it did not work out as expected and what you learned from it.

Sample answer: *Our CEO asked every department to send a representative to serve on the recruitment committee. It was thought that the more people involved, the better. It turned out to be a mess as each person had his or her own departmental priorities and expectations for how recruitment would take place. It was hard to come to a consensus on many things and time was wasted. I learned from the situation to request that a smaller team be assembled, that those who participate want to be there and that there should be a project leader to oversee a similar initiative.*

How do you delegate responsibility?

<u>Why this question is being asked</u>: As a supervisor, you are expected to delegate responsibility effectively, and the company wants to understand how you would do so.

<u>Strategy</u>: Provide clear insight into the process that you take in delegating responsibility and share a relevant example.

<u>Sample answer</u>: *I consider the strengths of my staff and their current responsibilities. I speak with each staff member, or a small team, about what I think they could take on and how I can support them. Once I feel that they are comfortable with the task and understand what is required, I pass it on to the project manager and provide regular check-ins and support.*

How do you feel about company politics?

<u>Why this question is being asked</u>: The interviewer is trying to gauge how much your work would be affected by internal politics taking place in the organization.

<u>Strategy</u>: Discuss how you would focus on the job and not get involved.

<u>Sample answer</u>: *I know that internal politics can have a negative impact on productivity so I do not get involved. I am the type of person who likes to focus on my work while I'm on the job.*

If you were CEO of this company, what would you change?

<u>Why this question is being asked</u>: To ascertain your understanding of the business and suggestions for improvement.

<u>Strategy</u>: Be cautious about providing too ambitious an answer so that you don't appear to be a "know it all". However, the interviewer does want an answer. Consider what changes the industry is undergoing at the moment and provide a suggestion that is relevant to trends in the field.

<u>Sample answer</u>: *As I have not sat in the CEO's chair before, I would not want to claim that I have an easy answer given today's difficult job market. From what I understand, many firms in this industry are converting to a technology based model and utilizing social media as an effective marketing tool. I feel that some resources can be shifted from the cold calling model towards this technology based model, and towards making customer experience with the technology model more interactive.*

Describe the relationship that should exist between a supervisor and those reporting to him/her.

Why this question is being asked: To understand both your management style as well as your ability to report to a supervisor.

Strategy: Describe the relationship as best you understand the management style that exists at the company. Describe a relationship that is one of mutual respect but where the lines of command are clearly delineated.

Sample answer: *The most important thing is to establish a relationship that is based on mutual respect. The subordinate has to respect the supervisor's ability to manage and the supervisor has to respect the employee. It should be a relationship where there is open communication between the parties. It is also important that each person knows their role and what is expected of them in order to meet objectives.*

Do you consider yourself a leader?

<u>Why this question is being asked</u>: To determine if you see leadership qualities in yourself.

<u>Strategy</u>: Make it clear that you do consider yourself a leader and provide a relevant example that proves it.

<u>Sample answer</u>: *I do consider myself a leader. I am always ready to share my expertise and provide counsel to those who are learning. When there is a new project or initiative underway, I have volunteered to take the lead and steer the project.*

Walk me through the important points on your resume.

Why this question is being asked: As the interviewer may not have had the opportunity to review your resume extensively before the interview, he/she would like to hear about the most important parts of your background.

Strategy: Don't tell your whole work or professional history but discuss the most salient points of your background.

Sample answer: *I've been in my last position since 2003. I lead a team of 20 sales agents. I have increased sales by 5-7% every year while cutting costs by 8-10% each year. I studied psychology in school and worked my way up from a sales coordinator in a niche firm to a management position in a Fortune 50 company. I am skilled in several database programs and Microsoft applications. I recently completed my masters in communications at Hudson University.*

Can you summarize the contribution you would make to our organization?

<u>Why this question is being asked</u>: To determine if you understand the position and the goals that the company would want met.

<u>Strategy</u>: Think back to what you've learned about the position and emphasize the goals that you would meet.

<u>Sample answer</u>: *In the role of call center manager, I would train reps. to effectively deal with customers and increase customer satisfaction. I would decrease time that customers spend on the phone by 25% and increase the satisfaction rate by a third. I would move us to a technology based model and allow us to cut down on the number of reps. that we require.*

What is the most difficult thing about working with you?

<u>Why this question is being asked</u>: To understand how you work with others.

<u>Strategy</u>: Focus on something that others might find challenging but is really a strength that you would bring to the company.

<u>Sample answer</u>: *I give 100% and I expect the same from others. I am very driven to succeed and I always give my all in providing the best work and getting things done well before the deadline.*

What major challenges and problems did you face in your last job?

<u>Why this question is being asked</u>: Jobs are full of challenges. The interviewer would like to know how you have handled problems or challenges in the past as you are likely to face obstacles in this job as well.

<u>Strategy</u>: Demonstrate how you can overcome a challenge. Provide an example of a problem or challenge that would have relevance for the interviewer and show how you overcame that challenge. In structuring your answer, provide the problem followed by the action and then the result.

<u>Sample answer</u>: *Two years ago, my employer acquired a niche firm. This created natural friction between long-time employees and those who came aboard during the acquisition. Each team had their own way of doing things. At the beginning, having more employees slowed down our ability to finish projects successfully due to miscommunication and conflict. After this happened, I asked members of our team to meet me for lunch. We went out in a relaxed atmosphere and began to discuss our working styles and why we work the way we do. It opened the line of communications and we began to understand each other better. This led to better teamwork in the future.*

Tell me about a time when you helped resolve a dispute between others.

<u>Why this question is being asked</u>: Conflicting opinions and strong personalities are often a part of the workplace. People that can take on leadership roles and resolve problems are heavily valued.

<u>Strategy</u>: Provide an example where you can demonstrate your leadership abilities to resolve a conflict. Explain what was the problem, the action that you took and the end result.

<u>Sample answer</u>: As *an accounts manager, I had taken on a mentoring role for two relatively new employees. They were working closely together, and a conflict arose as to which one should get the credit for securing the account. They agreed to talk it out with me before going to the supervisor. Upon hearing each other's side of the situation, they agreed that each deserved some credit and realized that to find mutual success in their new roles, they would be best served by working together.*

Tell me about an accomplishment you are most proud of.

<u>Why this question is being asked</u>: By learning about what you've accomplished in the past, the interviewer has a better sense of what you may accomplish in the future.

<u>Strategy</u>: Paint a picture with your words of an accomplishment that would be relevant to the position for which you are applying.

<u>Sample answer</u>: *I was called upon to do a job meant for two people. I was able not only to meet the demands of both positions, but to really excel. As the company acquired various new businesses, the CEO was looking for someone who already had experience in management to lead a new team. I was asked to do so while maintaining my old position as well. I would spend two and a half days at each site per week. Through maximizing resources, especially leaning on technology as a communication tool, I was able to stay on top of both roles and exceed expectations.*

Would you rather be liked or feared?

<u>Why this question is being asked</u>: The interviewer would like to get a better sense of your management style.

<u>Strategy</u>: Find a balance for a middle ground. If you only say that you want to be liked, the interviewer might think you are a pushover and if you say that you need to be feared, you'll come off as a dictator.

<u>Sample answer</u>: *I would want to be liked because I am a respected leader who leads by example. As an effective leader, my team would be fearful of not doing their best because each would know that everyone has put in a great effort and no one wants to disappoint the team.*

Give an example of a time you misjudged someone.

<u>Why this question is being asked:</u> Your ability to interact well with others is an essential aspect to success on a job.

<u>Strategy:</u> Provide clarity into why you misjudged a person, what happened as a result and how the issue was resolved.

<u>Sample answer:</u> *I try not to judge a person I don't know, but it can happen on occasion. When a new team, member joined our division, he seemed to be moving very fast to get noticed by our upper management. He set up meetings with the vice presidents and began giving reports on how we were operating. What I hadn't realized was that he was new to working in our industry and he didn't have a sense of the communication protocol that was established. Once he realized, he was quite embarrassed and became a better team player. He is actually quite humble and not looking to step over anyone.*

Why were you promoted?

<u>Why this question is being asked</u>: The interviewer would like to gain insight into how you were able to move up the corporate ladder.

<u>Strategy</u>: Discuss your accomplishments that lead to the promotion. Put a special focus on those accomplishments that would be relevant to the job.

<u>Sample answer</u>: *I was promoted from account manager to trainer within one year. This was due to my stellar record of sales while maintaining and growing accounts as well as my ability to lead others and train them to work effectively.*

What do you consider your most noteworthy accomplishment in your last job?

<u>Why this question is being asked</u>: To learn not only what you have done in a job but what you've actually accomplished.

<u>Strategy</u>: Provide an accomplishment related to the job you are interviewing for. Describe what needed to be done and how you went about doing it.

<u>Sample answer</u>: *When I started in the position, there was a great deal of infighting amongst the employees. Multiple people wanted to claim credit for the same things. I didn't feel that this was a good environment for working together and meeting our goals. I spoke with each employee about the culture and how things got to be the way they are and looked to change things slowly. I thought communication was a key and encouraged people to get together and talk as opposed to making assumptions or just sending an angry email. I organized two retreats a year so that we can work on our team building skills. Most importantly I continued to reinforce that we all needed to work together for everyone to benefit.*

Have you had experience firing people?

<u>Why this question is being asked</u>: If this is a function of the role, the interviewer wants to know if you have the stomach for it.

<u>Strategy</u>: If the answer is yes, provide insight into your process for undertaking that action.

<u>Sample answer</u>: *I have. It is never an easy process but in order for an organization to run efficiently, it has to be done sometimes. I am upfront with an employee when it is time as I don't want the person to feel uncertainty or allow for the possibility of rumors spreading as to the person's job status. It is important to provide feedback as to how he/she can improve in the future as well as provide resources so that he/she has a softer landing, such as outplacement services and a few weeks of severance pay.*

Describe your latest written communications and how effective it has been.

<u>Why this question is being asked</u>: To gain more insight into your communication skills based on a recent example.

<u>Strategy</u>: Focus on the positive impacts of a recent communication such as a press release or an internal memo explaining an important issue.

<u>Sample answer</u>: *There had been unfounded rumors that my employer was planning to lay off 20% of its workforce. Rather than writing a brief communication to try to squash a rumor, I wrote a longer communication explaining why it could not be true based on our current growth and our needs to continue to hire aggressively as opposed to laying people off.*

Describe a situation in which you led a team.

<u>Why this question is being asked</u>: Leadership abilities are an important element of most jobs.

<u>Strategy</u>: Provide an example of your leadership abilities that would be relevant to the job you are applying for.

<u>Sample answer</u>: *I was named the group leader for our expansion project. I was given the opportunity due to my history of meeting milestones and my ability to get along well with others. I really enjoyed the experience as I was able to train and support my peers. We all shined together as a team.*

Can you give me an example of your managerial skills?

<u>Why this question is being asked</u>: The interviewer wants to understand how you manage.

<u>Strategy</u>: Focus on a management skill that would be relevant for the job. Provide a story that would be memorable in demonstrating this skill.

<u>Sample answer</u>: *My skill is in rallying my team to work together. I had learned of some infighting between team members. I asked the whole team to get together and discuss what issues we were having and smooth out any problems. We dealt with the miscommunication and discussed how we could work together to meet objectives. The team did get on board and we completed the project successfully.*

What's the most difficult part of being a manager?

<u>Why this question is being asked</u>: The interviewer wants to consider what difficult parts of your current job might be relevant to the position you are applying for.

<u>Strategy</u>: Focus on a difficulty that you deal with that would be relevant to the position you are applying for. Explain how you overcome the challenge.

<u>Sample answer</u>: *It is a stomach churning experience to have to let people go. In the way I manage, I am looking for my company to run as effectively as possible. When we are doing that, we can help all of the employees at the company to support their families. From time to time, people no longer fit and we have to let them go in order to help the company to run as effectively as possible.*

Why have you had so many jobs?

<u>Why this question is being asked</u>: The interviewer wants to know how long you'll remain on the job and is concerned about your past.

<u>Strategy</u>: Focus on why this job would be a fit for you long term and why you had to move jobs in order to advance yourself.

<u>Sample answer</u>: *I have had to take risks to learn and advance myself in order to be in the position to compete for this job. Each opportunity was a great way for me to learn early in my career. I am now looking for a solid opportunity that I could grow in.*

Do you have the stomach to fire people?

<u>Why this question is being asked</u>: The interviewer wants to assess your ability to hold a management position and make difficult decisions.

<u>Strategy</u>: Prove that you can handle performing difficult responsibilities. Explain why you would be able to manage it.

<u>Sample answer</u>: *Well, in this role I know that I would have to make some difficult decisions. It is a stomach churning experience to have to fire people. When it doesn't feel like that any longer, someone probably shouldn't be doing it. In the way I manage, I am looking for my company to run as effectively as possible. When we are doing that, we can help all of the employees at the company to support their families. From time to time, people no longer fit and we have to let them go in order to help the company to run as effectively as possible.*

Describe a time when you took extra effort to make sure the person with whom you were communicating with had really understood your point.

<u>Why this question is being asked</u>: To determine if you are a good communicator.

<u>Strategy</u>: Provide an example relevant to your job where you solicited feedback from somebody to learn if he/she understood what you were asking.

<u>Sample answer</u>: *When I trained my sales team in some of the new techniques that we would be using, I asked them to role play a sales call utilizing the techniques. It was helpful in determining if they understood what I was asking for.*

Tell me about a time when you had to give someone difficult feedback and how you managed it.

<u>Why this question is being asked</u>: In a management role, or otherwise, you may have to have a discussion with a co-worker or subordinate that is a difficult one. The interviewer wants to understand how you would manage it.

<u>Strategy</u>: Provide a relevant example that explains the situation leading up to the conversation, what was said and what was the end result.

<u>Sample answer</u>: *It is never easy to provide someone with difficult feedback but in order to work most effectively, you just have to do it sometime. A salesperson who reported to me seemed like his hygiene habits had dropped off significantly. He went from wearing sharp suits to stained shirts, seemed like he often skipped showers and stopped shaving. I had a private conversation with him and mentioned how others had noticed that his habits had changed and became concerned. He explained that he was overwhelmed with his wife recently having children and it hadn't been on his radar as much as it had in the past. He said that he would take care of it. He did change the way that he dressed and cleaned himself up. I am glad that I told him as it probably would have cost him his job.*

Did you receive any promotions?

<u>Why this question is being asked</u>: The interviewer would like to look back on your history of achievement and advancement in order to properly gauge your potential for the future.

<u>Strategy</u>: If you do not have several examples, focus on one or two promotions that would be memorable for the interviewer to hear. Explain why you were deserving and what you accomplished when given the opportunity.

<u>Sample answer</u>: *I was named the group leader for our expansion project. I was given the opportunity due to my history of meeting milestones and my ability to get along well with others. I really enjoyed the experience as I was able to train and support my peers. We all shined together as a team.*

Describe a contribution you have made to a team project you worked on.

<u>Why this question is being asked</u>: Many assignments are expected to be completed collaboratively and the interviewer wants to learn about how you can contribute.

<u>Strategy</u>: Provide an example of a project that would be relevant to the job you are applying for.

<u>Sample answer</u>: *My team was responsible for creating a 360 degree competitor analysis report. I volunteered to do much of the heavy lifting in terms of data acquisition to allow my teammates to concentrate on further analyzing the information. I was also the person that gave the report its final polish and checked it for accuracy.*

What was the most important task you ever had?

<u>Why this question is being asked</u>: The interviewer wants to determine how you handle responsibility.

<u>Strategy</u>: Provide an example of a task that you handled that is relevant to the job and shows your ability to lead. Be sure to include what you accomplished.

<u>Sample answer</u>: *My firm gave me the responsibility of coordinating our volunteer efforts. Each member of our team is tasked with volunteering 100 hours each year. We had so much talent to work with that I didn't want their efforts to be wasted by working in a role that did not suit them. I reached out to 50 local non-profits and asked them to send me lists with descriptions of what volunteer opportunities they most needed to fill. I then met with my co-workers to determine what type of experience they were looking for to make the best match possible. It worked out great! Most people really enjoyed the volunteer experience and our CEO is thinking of expanding the volunteer hours next year as he feels that it improves office moral and when employers return to work, they are more productive.*

Do you check your messages while on vacation?

<u>Why this question is being asked</u>: The interviewer wants to know how well you maintain a work/life balance.

<u>Strategy</u>: Make it clear that you do stay in top of what is going on when you are away but that you are not a workaholic.

<u>Sample answer</u>: *Doesn't everybody? Sometimes things come up that have to be taken care of before I return. I try to check my phone and email messages at least once a day and either respond or delegate someone else to take care of the matter until I return.*

Give me an example from a previous job where you've shown initiative.

<u>Why this question is being asked</u>: Going beyond your responsibilities and taking initiative is a valued trait and the interviewer is looking to learn if you possess that inclination.

<u>Strategy</u>: Provide an example of a time that you took initiative that would be relevant to the job you are seeking. Clearly explain the reasons you took the initiative, what you did and what it ended up accomplishing.

<u>Sample answer</u>: *As our firm merged with a competitor, there was a lack of available employees to help train the staff that was newly acquired. I took the initiative to hold early am and lunch trainings to get them up to speed in things like using our database, communication protocols and sales processes.*

Explain how your work experience is relevant to this position.

<u>Why this question is being asked</u>: To understand your relevant experience for the position.

<u>Strategy</u>: Focus on the aspects of your experience that are most relevant to the position, whether you have had the actual job title before or not.

<u>Sample answer</u>: *All of my professional experience has relevance to this sales manager opportunity. In my sales and account manager roles I've taken on increased responsibility. I've also managed others in retail and food services environments, which has taught me to be a better manager.*

Would you work weekends?

<u>Why this question is being asked</u>: To get a sense of your schedule availability and commitment to the company.

<u>Strategy</u>: If it is the type of job where most of the business is on the weekends, such as retail or food services, the answer would have to be yes. If it is a job with traditional hours, make it clear that you would in special circumstances.

<u>Sample answer</u>: *I would be ready to pitch in when needed. As weekends are usually family time for me, I would like to stay on top of my work when things are busy by coming in early, working through lunch and staying late. I know during the busy season that it may not be enough time so I would come in when I am needed.*

Would you lie for the company?

<u>Why this question is being asked</u>: To get a sense of your moral compass.

<u>Strategy</u>: Make it clear that you would not lie.

<u>Sample answer</u>: *No, I could not lie for the company.*

Are you willing to relocate?

<u>Why this question is being asked</u>: If you are out of the area, the company wants to know if you are serious about the job and would relocate.

<u>Strategy</u>: Make it clear that your interest is genuine in the position and you have begun the exploratory stages to learn more about the area.

<u>Sample answer</u>: *Oh yes, I am very serious about considering this area for my next move. Along with flying in for the interview on Thursday, I've taken Friday off in order to get a better sense of the neighborhood, check out schools for my kids and learn more about the community.*

What do you find are the most difficult decisions to make?

<u>Why this question is being asked</u>: To learn about your decision making process.

<u>Strategy</u>: Consider the decisions that you would have to make in the role and use one as an example. Provide a reason why the decision might be difficult and how you would approach it.

<u>Sample answer</u>: *The most difficult decisions are the ones that affect the lives of people. Most decisions that an executive would make have a major impact on the lives of workers. I give much weight to this fact when considering the best course of action.*

What can you do for this company?

<u>Why this question is being asked</u>: To learn what your expectations are in contributing to the company.

<u>Strategy</u>: Demonstrate your knowledge of the needs of the company and the responsibilities of the position by giving a specific answer.

<u>Sample answer</u>: *As the operations manager, I would like to contribute to a more effective flow of processes and cost reduction for the company by implementing measures to improve shipping times and reduce the occurrence of goods becoming damaged in delivery. I would take some of the best practices that I learned over my career and partner with company management to learn the methods that work best here.*

How would you show your team the importance of cooperation?

<u>Why this question is being asked:</u> Being able to work effectively with those who report to you is an essential tool.

<u>Strategy</u>: Use an example relevant to the job that demonstrates your ability to get your team to work together.

<u>Sample answer</u>: *I am a data driven person and I would create a chart that compares what we can do separately compared to what we could accomplish together to meet objectives. It is hard to think outside of ourselves, but when a person sees a visual of how he/she can work most effectively in a group, it is memorable.*

When you are on vacation, what do you miss most about your work?

Why this question is being asked: To see how you will describe your job when you are on a break.

Strategy: Be positive but be careful to avoid seeming disingenuous. You won't be taken seriously if you say you miss absolutely everything. Provide one example that would be relevant to the job you are interviewing for.

Sample answer: *Although it is a demanding environment, I get used to the hustle and bustle of the work week and I do miss it, somewhat, when I am away. My vacations are usually just a few short days here and there so thankfully I don't have to miss work too much.*

What did you like most about the kind of jobs you held in the past?

<u>Why this question is being asked</u>: To understand what type of work gives you satisfaction and why.

<u>Strategy</u>: Focus on the progressive nature of each opportunity. Give examples that would be relevant to this job.

<u>Sample answer</u>: *The thing that I enjoyed most about the jobs I've held in the past is the opportunity to take on additional responsibilities as I learned. For example, in my first job I learned the business and within two years, I was training others.*

Do you participate in many social activities with your team?

<u>Why this question is being asked</u>: The interviewer wants to understand what type of team player you are and your balance of work/life.

<u>Strategy</u>: Demonstrate that you are a team player and know that it is important to participate in order to build a good rapport but that you have to balance it with your personal life as well.

<u>Sample answer</u>: *I do participate in some. It is a good opportunity to get to know my team outside of a work situation. I wouldn't say that I participate in many but we do go out regularly, about once a month.*

What social obligations go along with a job in this field?

<u>Why this question is being asked</u>: The interviewer wants to know if you understand the business and demands on your time outside traditional hours.

<u>Strategy</u>: Demonstrate your knowledge of the social obligations required outside the 9 to 5.

<u>Sample answer</u>: *I know that social situations are a great way to network and there are many opportunities to grow business by attending regular local meet ups and the occasional regional convention. I am ready to commit to these types of events as I know that they are crucial to success.*

How does your present position differ from past ones?

<u>Why this question is being asked</u>: The interviewer wants to understand if you've grown in your career or stood still.

<u>Strategy</u>: Focus on the additional responsibilities you've taken on and how you've grown.

<u>Sample answer</u>: *My present position has been a great opportunity to utilize all of the knowledge that I've acquired in the past. I have taken on the additional responsibility of becoming a team leader, the first time that I've been in a management role.*

How did your last job influence your career?

<u>Why this question is being asked</u>: The interviewer wants to understand how you learn from each situation and what influence that has had on you now.

<u>Strategy</u>: Focus on aspects of what you've learned that would be helpful to the job you are interviewing for. Provide relevant examples to back up what you are explaining.

<u>Sample answer</u>: *My last job allowed me to take on more management responsibilities and that has influenced my ability to take on a full-time role as a manager. I was able to lead a team under tight deadlines to exceed management expectations.*

How many hours do you normally work?

<u>Why this question is being asked</u>: The interviewer wants to know how seriously you take your work and what you are willing to do to complete it.

<u>Strategy</u>: Paint a picture of someone who is willing to do whatever is necessary to complete the work but not of a workaholic.

<u>Sample answer</u>: *Beyond the typical nine-to-five 40 hour work week, I put in as many hours as necessary to complete my work. During a quieter time of year, it may only be 40 or 45 hours a week. When it is our busier season, it may be 50-60, really depending on what needs to get done.*

Do you take work home with you?

<u>Why this question is being asked</u>: The interviewer wants to know how seriously you take your work and what you are willing to do to complete it.

<u>Strategy</u>: Paint a picture of someone who is willing to do whatever is necessary to complete the work but not of a workaholic.

<u>Sample answer</u>: *I do when it is necessary. I try to plan my schedule with my goals prioritized so that I can give myself enough time to complete everything before a deadline approaches. As that is not always possible, I try to come in early or work through lunch when necessary. If work still needs to get completed, I'll bring it on the train or work on it once my family has gone to sleep.*

Tell me about your most significant work experience.

<u>Why this question is being asked</u>: The interviewer wants to gain greater insight into your previous work experience to understand how you might do on a job in the future.

<u>Strategy</u>: Focus on a work experience that is relevant to the position you are applying for.

<u>Sample answer</u>: *Similar to this position, I served as a process manager for five years. I oversaw the work of 7 employees. We reduced inefficiency by a 30% average each year.*

What systems would you put in place to enable employees to give management suggestions?

<u>Why this question is being asked</u>: To understand your process for receiving employee feedback.

<u>Strategy</u>: Demonstrate that you are the type of manager who would welcome employee feedback and the systems that you would put in place. Include a few possibilities to account for various forms of feedback.

<u>Sample answer</u>: *I think that employee feedback is essential as these are the people on the ground who can give you the best suggestions. Some employees are intimidated, or fear reprisal, no matter how much you say that you are open to feedback. It is important to have multiple ways to gain insight. I have an open door policy where employees can speak to me at anytime. Employees are encouraged to email me suggestions and we have a website submission form for those that want to remain anonymous.*

What qualities make you a good leader?

<u>Why this question is being asked</u>: To learn what qualities you have that make you fit for leadership.

<u>Strategy</u>: Provide a handful of relevant qualities and explain why those make you a good leader.

<u>Sample answer</u>: *I lead by example. I wouldn't ask my team to do anything that I wouldn't do. I am resourceful. I can work within a budget and time constraints to get the job done. I am also a natural teacher. I am patient and enjoy teaching people ways to work more effectively.*

This job has a large component of negotiation. How will you deal with that?

<u>Why this question is being asked</u>: To learn if you can handle negotiation as an essential aspect of the job.

<u>Strategy</u>: Explain your strategy for managing negotiation as a part of your job. Provide a relevant example of how you have handled negotiation in the past.

<u>Sample answer</u>: *I enjoy the art of negotiation. I believe in creating a win-win scenario in any form of negotiation. When someone sees that you are approaching the negotiation process in good faith, it is easier to build rapport and begin serious negotiations. In my last role, I was responsible for negotiating a new union contract. I was open with the union reps in showing them our books over the last five years so that they could see that we were not earning the profits that they expected and why we should look towards a 1% raise instead of their 5% demand. We ended up at a 1.5% increase.*

ABOUT THE AUTHOR

Lavie Margolin is the author of Winning Answers to 500 Interview Questions, an Amazon Kindle #1 Best Seller for Job Interviewing. He founded LCJS consulting in 2003. Lavie uses his background in marketing and adult learning, his expert knowledge of LinkedIn and over a decade of experience in career coaching to help individuals and businesses identify and reach their goals. Lavie holds a B.S. degree in Marketing from Yeshiva University and an MA in adult learning at SUNY Empire State.

You can contact Lavie Margolin via the following methods:

Phone: (845) 480-2823

Email: Laviemarg@Lioncubjobsearch.com

Twitter: @Laviemarg

LinkedIn:http://www.linkedin.com/in/laviemargolin

Each book review posted on Amazon allows potential readers to determine if this is the book for them. Would you be so kind as to post your candid review of this book on Amazon?

Made in the USA
Monee, IL
27 September 2022